22.60

EDGE
BOOKS

X-Sports
KICKBOXING

BY TERRI SIEVERT

CONSULTANT:
MIKE MILES
NATIONAL KICKBOXING & MUAY THAI
CALGARY, CANADA

Capstone
press
Mankato, Minnesota

Edge Books are published by Capstone Press
151 Good Counsel Drive, P.O. Box 669, Mankato, Minnesota 56002
www.capstonepress.com

Library of Congress Cataloging-in-Publication Data
Sievert, Terri.
    Kickboxing / by Terri Sievert.
    p. cm.—(Edge books. X-sports)
    Includes bibliographical references and index.
    ISBN 0-7368-2710-2 (hardcover)
    1. Kickboxing—Juvenile literature. I. Title. II. Series.
GV1114.65.S54 2005
796.815—dc22   2004001732

Summary: Discusses the sport of kickboxing, including gear needed, punches and kicks,
    and famous kickboxers.

Editorial Credits
Tom Adamson, editor; Jason Knudson, designer and illustrator; Jo Miller,
    photo researcher; Eric Kudalis, product planning editor

Photo Credits
Corbis/Reuters NewMedia Inc., 14; TempSport/Franck Seguin, 5, 6, 13 (top), 17, 19,
    20 (both), 23; Bettmann, 27
Getty Images/AFP/Mehdi Fedouach, cover; Mike Powell, 9; John Gichigi, 11,
    13 (bottom), 18
Zuma Press/Mary Ann Owen, 28

1 2 3 4 5 6 09 08 07 06 05 04

TABLE OF CONTENTS

CHAPTER 1:
Kickboxing 4

CHAPTER 2:
Kickboxing Gear 10

CHAPTER 3:
Kickboxing Moves 16

CHAPTER 4:
Martial Arts Pros 26

How to Do a Side Kick 24

Glossary 30

Read More 31

Internet Sites 31

Index 32

KICKBOXING

The champion kickboxer jabs the challenger. He then hits the challenger with a cross punch. The champion turns and brings his leg up for a powerful kick. The challenger tries to block the attack. He bounces off the ropes. The champion takes advantage of his opponent being off balance. He hits him with a fast roundhouse kick that knocks the wind out of him.

Kickboxers punch like boxers. They use kicks from martial arts, such as karate, kung fu, tae kwon do, and Muay Thai. Fighters need to be strong and fit. Good fighters have discipline and control. Doing the moves quickly and correctly is as important as having muscle power.

LEARN ABOUT:

- Martial arts influence
- Full-contact karate
- Muay Thai

Kickboxing is full of intense, hard-hitting action.

Some styles of kickboxing allow leg kicks.

TYPES OF KICKBOXING

Different types of kickboxing are popular. Some fighters compete in full-contact karate or international rules kickboxing matches. Others do Muay Thai, or Thai kickboxing. Each form of the sport has its own rules.

Full-contact karate is the most popular form of kickboxing in the United States. Fighters must land punches and kicks above the waist. They cannot use their knees and elbows to strike an opponent. Fighters must use at least eight kicks in each round of a fight.

In international rules kickboxing, fighters can use a kick into the thigh. They do not need to use a certain number of kicks in each round. Pro fighters do not need to wear shin or foot pads. Amateur athletes do wear shin pads.

Muay Thai is a style of fighting from Thailand. In North America, Thai kickboxers can hit any part of the leg except the knee. In other parts of the world, Muay Thai allows the knee as a target. Thai fighters can use a knee to hit an opponent's body. In some matches, they can hit an opponent's head with the knee. Elbow strikes are allowed in some matches. Pro Thai kickboxers cannot wear shin and foot pads.

KICKBOXING HISTORY

Kickboxing was first known as full-contact karate. Karate did not allow opponents to hit each other. Fighters wanted a sport that let them strike an opponent. In the 1970s, they combined kicks and punches. Fighters liked this style of fighting. Soon, safety gear was developed to lower the chance of injury. The sport quickly became popular.

Thai kickboxing allows elbow strikes in some matches.

EDGE FACT

Cardio kickboxing is used as a workout routine. Cardio kickboxers use kicks and punches to stay fit. They do not fight against an opponent.

CHAPTER 2

KICKBOXING GEAR

Kickboxers wear boxing gloves. Mouthpieces and groin guards help prevent injury. Some kickboxers wear headgear. Kickboxers wear baggy pants or kickboxing shorts. Women also wear a shirt or tank top.

PADS AND GLOVES

Some kickboxing styles require pads on the feet and legs. Foot pads protect a kickboxer's toes and the top of the foot. Shin pads cover the front of the shin. The pads shield the shin from painful kicks. The soft pads are held in place with straps around the foot and leg. The pads are made of foam and covered in vinyl.

LEARN ABOUT:
- Gloves
- Punching bags
- Focus pads

In some events, kickboxers wear foot pads.

Kickboxers wear gloves to protect their hands. The size of glove the fighter wears depends on body weight. Heavy kickboxers wear heavy gloves.

Smaller gloves are used for hitting punching bags. These gloves are lightweight and have extra padding for the knuckles. Larger gloves with extra padding are used for sparring. Sparring gloves fit tightly around a fighter's wrist.

Hand wraps also protect fighters' hands. They give extra support to the fingers and wrists. A fighter's hands are wrapped in a cotton bandage or gauze and tape for a competition.

HEAD PROTECTION

Headgear guards a kickboxer's jaw and chin. It also protects the back of the head. It adjusts to fit to head size but should not block vision. Headgear is made of leather or foam. The padding absorbs hits to the head. Pro kickboxers are not required to wear headgear.

Kickboxers use boxing gloves.

Kickboxers wear hand wraps under their gloves.

A mouthpiece is fitted to the shape of a kickboxer's teeth. Without a mouthpiece, a kickboxer could have teeth knocked out or bite off part of the tongue.

TRAINING

Kickboxers need to train. They must have stamina. They do not want to get tired during a match. They increase stamina by running, punching or kicking a bag, and shadowboxing.

Kickboxers train with Thai pads or focus pads.

Different gear is used when a kickboxer trains. Catching a large and heavy medicine ball helps a fighter practice taking a hit. Lifting weights makes kickboxers stronger.

PUNCHING BAGS

Punching bags help kickboxers train. Punching bags come in different shapes and sizes. A banana bag is 6 to 7 feet (1.8 to 2.1 meters) long. It weighs 200 pounds (91 kilograms). The smaller chaser bag bobs quickly from side to side. Punching bags can be filled with water or cloth.

A trainer may wear focus pads or focus mitts to help kickboxers learn to hit a target. The round focus pads are hard and have a flat surface. The trainer slips the hands into straps on the back to hold the focus pads.

Trainers use other types of pads. A trainer can wear Thai pads. Thai pads are larger than focus pads and are shaped like a rectangle. A trainer holds a kicking shield to help a fighter practice kicks. The shield is 8 to 12 inches (20 to 30 centimeters) thick.

CHAPTER 3

KICKBOXING MOVES

The best way to learn kickboxing moves is from a trainer. Kickboxers practice with a sparring partner and punching bag. The sparring partner practices blocking light, controlled blows from a partner. Heavy blows are saved for the punching bag. Sparring is supervised to make sure no one gets hurt.

A kickboxer starts in the fighting stance. For a right-handed fighter, the left foot is forward. The right foot is turned slightly to the right. It's the other way for left-handed fighters. The feet are shoulder width apart. The fists are in front of the face. Arms are bent with elbows in.

LEARN ABOUT:
- Fighting stance
- Punches and kicks
- Blocking

The fighting stance is the kickboxer's ready position.

A kickboxer must use well-placed, quick punches.

PUNCHES

Kickboxers use different kinds of punches. A jab is a quick hit. The fighter uses the knuckles of the middle and index fingers. The fist snaps out and back. The palm is facing down.

A cross is a punch straight at the opponent. A kickboxer turns the shoulders and hips. The kickboxer pivots on the ball of the rear foot when striking. A jab followed by a cross is a powerful combination.

A fighter pulls the shoulder back to hit with a hook. The elbow is up, and the arm goes across the body. The body, shoulders, and hips twist inward as the punch is thrown. The fighter's weight shifts to the front leg.

A spinning backfist is a flashy kickboxing move. The fighter turns to the right while spinning the head around to look at the opponent. The right arm whips straight out. The opponent gets hit with the back of the fist.

A kickboxer uses an uppercut to strike the opponent's chin.

The side kick strikes an opponent with the heel.

The roundhouse kick can be a powerful weapon.

KICKS

Kicks are fast and powerful. A kickboxer can hit a target with the ball of the foot, heel, top part of the foot, or shin. Eyes look forward at the target when a kick is thrown.

A kickboxer begins most kicks by lifting the knee to the chest. This move is called chambering. It gives a fighter more balance and protection.

The side kick is a basic kickboxing move. It's used for offense or defense. From a fighting stance, a fighter turns forward and chambers the leg. The fighter turns to the left as the foot is turned out. The knee points to the side. The leg is extended and rechambered. The target is hit with the heel.

With a hook kick, a kickboxer uses the heel as a weapon. The fighter raises the leg like a side kick. But the leg hooks to one side just before hitting the target.

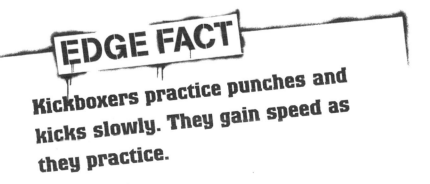

EDGE FACT

Kickboxers practice punches and kicks slowly. They gain speed as they practice.

THE ROUNDHOUSE

A rear-leg roundhouse kick can strike an opponent with the instep or ball of the foot. The right leg is chambered. The body turns to the left and the kicking leg extends. The right leg swings at the opponent with a powerful snap. The fighter returns to the fighting stance. The roundhouse can also be done with the front leg. A fighter can use the roundhouse to hit an opponent's legs.

The roundhouse can use the shin as a weapon. When a fighter does a shin roundhouse, the chambering move is not needed.

BLOCKING THE BLOWS

A fighter may try to catch a punch or kick to stop it. The fighter stops the blow with the rear hand. Weight shifts to the back leg.

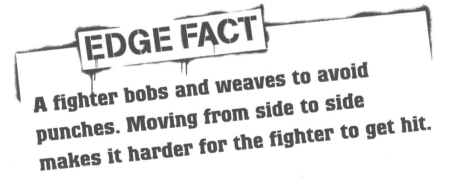

EDGE FACT

A fighter bobs and weaves to avoid punches. Moving from side to side makes it harder for the fighter to get hit.

A bent knee can block low kicks. A kick can also be blocked with the arm. The left arm is bent with the fist near the neck. It straightens down to block the kick.

A fighter can also redirect a punch or kick. Instead of stopping the blow, they knock the blow aside to avoid getting hit.

A fighter can block a high kick with the gloves.

HOW TO DO A
SIDE KICK

1. The fighter begins in the fighting stance, then chambers the right leg.

2. The fighter turns the hips to the left but keeps looking at the opponent.

24

3. The kicking leg extends quickly to strike the opponent.

4. The fighter brings the leg back to the chamber position, then returns to the fighting stance.

CHAPTER 4

MARTIAL ARTS PROS

Jhoon Rhee brought tae kwon do to the United States in the 1950s. He influenced the development of full-contact karate in the 1970s. He also invented safety gear for karate. He has a series of tae kwon do schools. He also gives motivational speeches.

Bruce Lee was a famous action movie star. He made up his own style of fighting called Jeet Kune Do. It combined martial arts kicks, boxing, wrestling, and judo. He's thought to be the first person to combine styles to invent a new martial art. He helped make martial arts popular in the United States.

LEARN ABOUT:
- Jhoon Rhee and Bruce Lee
- Superfoot
- Maurice Smith

Bruce Lee made the martial arts popular in the United States with his action movies.

Maurice Smith has intimidated opponents for more than 20 years.

28

KICKBOXING STARS

Bill "Superfoot" Wallace was a kickboxing star in the 1970s. He had a quick left leg. He could kick as fast he could punch.

Grace Casillas was a champion kickboxer in the 1980s. She acted in TV shows and films. She was also a boxer and martial arts teacher.

Kathy Long is known for her spinning backfist. She only lost one match as a pro kickboxer. She left kickboxing in the 1990s to become a pro boxer.

Maurice Smith has been a top kickboxer for more than 20 years. He has been a world heavyweight kickboxing champion. He has fought in all types of kickboxing. He also works to promote the sport and helps kickboxing continue to grow in popularity.

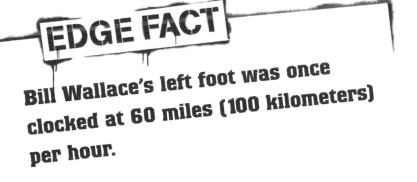

EDGE FACT

Bill Wallace's left foot was once clocked at 60 miles (100 kilometers) per hour.

GLOSSARY

martial arts (MAR-shuhl ARTS)—styles of self-defense and fighting; tae kwon do, judo, and karate are examples of martial arts.

medicine ball (MED-uh-suhn BAHL)—a heavy, stuffed ball used to train for kickboxing; people play catch with the heavy ball.

pivot (PIV-uht)—to turn on a central point

shadowboxing (SHAD-oh-boks-ing)—punching the air against a pretend opponent

sparring (SPAR-ing)—practicing punches and kicks with a partner with light and controlled contact

stamina (STAM-uh-nuh)—the energy and strength to keep doing something for a long time

vinyl (VYE-nuhl)—a soft, shiny plastic

READ MORE

Chesterman, Barnaby. *Taekwondo*. Martial and Fighting Arts. Broomall, Penn.: Mason Crest, 2003.

Collins, Paul. *Muay Thai: Thai Boxing*. Martial Arts. Broomall, Penn.: Chelsea House, 2002.

Johnson, Nathan. *Kickboxing*. Martial and Fighting Arts. Broomall, Penn.: Mason Crest, 2003.

Scandiffio, Laura. *The Martial Arts Book*. Toronto: Annick Press, 2003.

INTERNET SITES

FactHound offers a safe, fun way to find Internet sites related to this book. All of the sites on FactHound have been researched by our staff.

Here's how:

1. Visit *www.facthound.com*
2. Type in this special code **0736827102** for age-appropriate sites. Or enter a search word related to this book for a more general search.
3. Click on the **Fetch It** button.

FactHound will fetch the best sites for you!

INDEX

blocking, 22–23

Casillas, Grace, 29
chambering, 21, 22

fighting stance, 16
focus pads, 15
foot pads, 7, 8, 10
full-contact karate, 7,
    8, 26

gloves, 10, 12

hand wraps, 12
headgear, 10, 12

international rules
    kickboxing, 7

karate, 4, 8, 26
kicks
    hook kick, 21
    roundhouse, 4, 22
    side kick, 21

Lee, Bruce, 26
Long, Kathy, 29

mouthpieces, 10, 14
Muay Thai, 4, 7, 8

punches
    cross, 4, 18
    hook, 19
    jab, 4, 18
    spinning backfist, 19,
        29
punching bags, 12,
    14–15, 16

Rhee, Jhoon, 26

safety gear, 8, 10, 12, 14
Smith, Maurice, 29
sparring, 12, 16

tae kwon do, 4, 26
training, 14–15

Wallace, Bill "Superfoot,"
    29